Daydreams on Venus

Love, Loneliness, & Life Lessons
with Jade Leonard

Wider Perspectives Publishing ¤ 2021 ¤ Norfolk, Va

Wider Perspectives Publishing, Norfolk, Va
ISBN: 978-1-952773-48-8

Meet Your Poet

A Georgia native residing in Norfolk, Virginia, Jade is an Entrepreneur at heart who longs for existential peace and happiness, and loves writing. She pours her heart onto pages to the rhythm in her mind when she can't find the words to speak. Among other creative and social achievements, Jade, age 25, has already shown a promising future as one of Hampton Roads newest business owners, providing numerous media related services and opportunities to include, CEO of Jade Leo Media (JLM), The UpNext Editor-In-Chief, and Norfolk Gems Co-Founder, a volunteering community organization.

This book is for the hopeful romantics who tend to romanticize life; the intense creatives and lovers of profound words; the humans going through a struggle, yet optimistic and wanting to develop personally. Enjoy!

"I've escaped to my own world. It's safe and has all the things I need. But one thing I can't escape is the memories made. Even though I've planted seeds. There's no place for growth in your comfort zone."

Follow Jade online
Website: jadeleomedia.com
Business Instagram: @jadeleomedia
Instagram : @rare.gem__

Contents

LOVE

I've escaped to my own world.
It's safe and has all the things I need.

Out of this World

Your enticing love gets me high
Take me to the moon
forget the sky
I love you when you look into my eyes
I stay there and time seems to fly by
Don't leave me in the morning, I hate to watch you go.
Where are you going? I want to know!
Take me with you, let's make this last.
Not just some girl of the past.
You know the real me, not many do.
If I know the real you can he stay too?
I trace your body in the night, my love, I adore you....
I'd do anything for you.

Daydreams on Venus

Good Lips

He's such a good kisser
Wanna make him my mister
Tender, plump, and juicy as fuck
every time gets sweeter
I could kiss em' forever
Its like his lips were made for mine
The experience is purely divine
Forehead, lip, neck, nipples, I love all of em'
I feel so good when we're together
He holds me through the stormy weather
I love it when I make him laugh
Wish these moments could forever last
He's a good indicator of how I've moved on from the past
It's not perfect and I still have a ways to go
he's not mine, belongin' to the streets
So I'll play my role
Which isn't an easy feat
But he teaches me
Patience and letting go of what I can't control
Today, for once I wasn't sad to see him go
Usually, my heart feels so low
But there's good in tomorrow
I'm learning to love me and spending time with myself more wisely
I'll see him when I see him and I kinda like it
No chasing him down, blowing up his phone,
wondering when he'll reach out to me next
At some point I had to take my power back
The Vitamin D he provides keeps me attracted
It fits just right and leaves me happy
I be movin' too fast, he didn't even ask for it

Didn't even hint it

But I just had to be about some action
Sure I was a lil' aroused the 2nd time around,
but that doesn't mean he'll stick around
Sometimes we cuddle
other times we'll go our separate ways
But I still feel him close to me anyways
There may not be a romantic future but he said we'll always be friends
Something about that statement makes me feel okay
I don't know where its going but I must keep my options open
Putting all my eggs in this basket; I'll make my way to an early casket
There is some value I've yet to fully see it but
When the time comes I'll know when I need to make my exit

Out of Sight, In my Mind

They say out of sight out of mind
but absence makes the heart grow fonder
I loved you more but I can't take this any longer
but you stayed in my mind,
always existing
I feel like you were my first love
but lust poses like love's sister
name should've been Eve the way I bit into the poisonous apple,
I just knew, one day I'd stare you down in a chapel
But we kissed and said goodbye
and that's how I want it to stay,
no sending random texts talkin' bout some "hey.. how you doing?....
hope all is well"...
we both know in our hearts that shit is superficial as hell
we got this, we can do it, gotta play by new rules,
and yo I'm just really done lookin' like your fool
I know you care about me, but it's just not enough,
leaving you is tough
but what's done gotta be done.
you'll forever have a piece of me,
you were always there in time of need,
but now it's time to set me free
Let me go and spread my wings
I know you got this, you're your own man,
if you really wanted me I'd have a ring on my left hand
I know you understand, gotta be the best version of me,
Gotta look up instead of down at my feet

But my path is golden, gonna keep looking ahead
my heart will be unfrozen I don't wanna be sad,
I refuse to cry, I know 1 one of these days I'll be ready for another guy
you'll meet a girl and sweep her off her feet,
I'll be happy for you, I pray you do the same for me

But don't get it twisted, I'm the who got away,
have you thinking "damn I shoulda gave shawty everything"
but never mind that, we're in different places now,
we both learned lessons and now time's run out
my last night with you, there were stars in my eyes,
but even starry nights have the darkest skies.
I'll see you again
this won't be forever,
and when that day comes,
never say never.

The Porch

It's time to let go
It hurts me so
I keep my actions to myself
The breeze I felt
From our dynamic that's shifting
Forever straddling the friend lover boundary
It's time to pick a side
I've made mine?
Even though I wanna call you late past 9
My higher self is saying don't turn back now
Ringing on a bell to a door that's not my house
a home that's not mine
Faulty roof, broken doors
no lights on inside
Shivering on the porch but no one to let me in
Still I stand firm and look past all the damage

Siren

I show them heaven but give em hell
I sure know how to lure them in
like a siren catching sailors
Enchantingly singing men to the rocks
Drawing them in with my beauty and song
Just waiting to eat their hearts out all along

Till there's nothing left
Only bones and flesh
Shred apart their hairy chest
Damn why did I do that?
Waiting till they come again
Store em in my cheek
Just in case I need to feed

Boys so so scrumptious
Oh so delicious
Tasty for a while
Get bored then
closed out like a case file
Or just lead them
Straight to the water
Can't make em drink it
But they'll dip both their feet in

Beautiful to gaze at
Beautiful from afar
Blazing inside
internally scarred
Valleys and ranges of magma-filled mountains.
Bubbling and spilling over to rivers and fountains
All covered beneath the surface with bright eyes and a smile
Girl, how are you? Are you okay?

Yea I'm fine— just good ol' denial

Shelve the pain
To the rear of my brain
It hurts so much I'll never say a thing
Then you hit a certain button
And didn't even know it
Now the bull is charging ahead
Horns fully out, smoke's coming out of my head
All I see is red, zero to a hundred
Be careful with this beauty your heart may plummet

Perfect Storm

I think he runs me
I Can't let him run me
Why it always gotta be on your time?
Why ya always gotta b line?

That question
That comment
or statement
Out the door and onto the pavement

I don't wanna like you
Really don't want to like you
If I get too close
Then I'll just drown

Got goggles on my face
Can't see, won't hear a sound
Smiling on my face and
extremely overwhelmed

Feelings pushing on me
But I just fight back
They're bubbling over,
got me feeling sick
Can't say what you want to hear
Yea, you're not gonna like that

Can't get too close to you
Can't share my true feelings
Can't want too much
Can't stay away

Barely Holding the balance
Really feeling the weight
Can't change ya to save the world
Can't change the world to be ya girl
There's still so much I don't say
I know I can't make you stay.
if it's over let's trade mistakes
please don't look at me that way
I could love you just not today

Lover & Dreamer

He changes with the seasons
She brings him to the ground
asking him to smell the roses
covered all around

He'd rather daydream
lifted in the clouds
That's fun for a while
Yet that's not her style

At heart, she's super practical
His nature's pure romantic
The lover can't help but fall for his
little charming antics

The pedestal he built is fit for a queen
Squeaky clean, shiny, and pristine
When they're together it's hot & exotic
As she's the most sensual and he the most erotic

The lover enjoys the touches and tender neck kisses
The bites, the bruises, the subtle bend to submission
But in reality, it was just a vision

Loneliness

One thing I can't escape is the memories made,
even though I've planted seeds,

Twiddle Dumb

I want to lend and not borrow
Never expect anything in return
Sitting here alone when I'd rather be with you
If actions speak louder than words
Then I should've got a clue
This ain't new
The lack of Communication
The no expectations
leaves me empty and wasted
Times wasted
When I should be developing myself
Making me a better me
instead of worried about everyone else
Versus thinking 'bout what could be
'Tween you and I
To myself I lied
Gonna wipe my eye
Before I even cry
Solidify the absolution that love will die
Before it even started
Barely in bloom
Gotta keep one foot out the door
So it'll lessen the doom

Whole Heartedly

I want to love someone so much
But why can't I love myself enough?
I appreciate the person I'm becoming
Starting to love the person I'm becoming
But then I have times where my soul feels empty and I'm completely alone
I can be alone all the time and feel perfectly fine
but other days I feel lonely and desperate
and I don't know what I need or what food I eat ...
so I lay in bed flipping through TV
Feeling nothing close to deserving
Feeling kinda sorry for myself for no reason at all
I'm the one who cut everyone off
I'm the one who decided to separate myself for what I thought was good reason
But there are people showing up in this season
but they can't fulfill my needs or fill the void that's so apparent
in my demeanor ... if you could see her
Drowning in despair like the snake eating its on tail
I thought I was doing great? What changed? Was it all a lie?
Am I that delusional I convinced myself I'm fine?
I thought I was making strides in this life
Reversing the damage that piled up for years,
mining away at the build-up of disappointments and fears
What was done to me by men, friends and family
Trying to handle it on my own and kept my lips tight
With every fight, kept my walls up with all my might
I've been treated so badly by people who were supposed to love me
and, like a child I always love them back no matter how they cut me
no matter what went wrong 'cuz at the end of the day it's my song

Daydreams on Venus

A Rock in a Safe Space

Feeling stuck I'm in a rut
And my mind won't change
Tryna see the (program) through
And stay in my lane
I feel like I'm the blame
Carry all this Shame
Back from my younger days
Aching to change
 the future
Stuck in a cube
with a computer
Went after the Money so I can't complain
But I do anyway I feel like I'm the blame
Built around security and material possessions
Don't think that I could fork the struggle
Wanna dig deep in my obsessions
This career is a curse yet a blessing

Daydreams on Venus

Jade Leonard

Papercuts

Lending pieces of my heart out just for it to be broken, torn, shredded, mistreated,
Neglected, crumbled, forgotten, lost, and anything else you could think of that happens to paper,
That's why I'm waiting for "the one" to give my whole heart too
But is that just a myth at this point? Or just pure fantasy?
Waiting for my hero to rescue me? Can't a girl dream?
But I can't sleep too long and lately
I feel like that's all I've been doing.
Waiting for the green light to hit the gas pedal to keep moving.
I gotta wake up and smell the roses,
but the roses have been in front of my face the whole time
just never noticed.
Trying to love me so hard who knew it would take this long?
I want everything right now and yet nothing at all.
If I died today I'd be small.
So I live for today 'cuz I can't take it when I'm gone.
To be 20 something is a blessing and curse.
Trying not to be selfish by putting yourself 1st.
So many lessons learned and many to go.
I wish my future self could tell me now what I should know.

Daydreams on Venus

Focus on Me

Focus on me
Crave my attention
Don't ignore me
I want Someone attentive
If you chill with me gotta know how to relax
No distractions
be receptive
To what I offer
and present in the moment
Gotta be confident and trust in yourself
Accept the person you are and fully capable
Gotta like what I see and have that chemistry
2 things that are priority
Get close to me and show me what's intimacy
What I have and faced in the past
Expectations unmet and not taken care of
I blame my daddy for these dramatics
Hella selfish and emotionally absent
I feel abandoned, no relationship can withstand it,
fearful in many ways I didn't even know it
no matter how much I laugh I still can never hide it
Like the Scarlett letter vividly red across my chest,
this hurt is so embedded

Daydreams on Venus

Push and Pull

I feel like my soul is pulling back and forth. I feel like I have to be someone I'm not in order to fit in or "make a good impression" and for what? A good evaluation?
There's more to life than that. I chose it but I chose wrong.
This is the bed I have to lay in and it feels so uncomfortable.
I want out of this so bad. But I feel like there's nothing I can do.
I feel like I don't have a place anywhere but I don't feel like I have many options to change it.
I just want to jump without a care if I fall or land. Anything different would feel good to me right about now. But I have that lingering thought of making the wrong decision and taking this life that I have so good for granted. I don't care about the brownie points, the ratings. When will I be satisfied? How come it's never enough? I just know I'm supposed to be somewhere else.
But I don't know what direction I'm supposed to go in. So I feel like I have to stay put and it hurts because of my need for independence and creativity.
Change is bursting at the seams. I can't compare that'll never do me any good.

Grounded

Looks can be deceiving when one is blessed with such beauty
This well runs deep if you'd bother to scratch the surface
I'll get to know you, but who wants to know me?
Stretching my energy, it can be exhausting.
Expectations built, which end up falling
So much pressure around my "true calling"
This planet has its shadows
but she's the brightest star in the galaxy.
Just as down as Earth-- grounded and sturdy.

Life Lessons

Even though I've planted seeds,
there's no place for growth in your comfort zone.

Relentless

I set the boundary
I've said my piece
I've drawn the line
Now it's time to fall inline
And if you don't, that's completely fine
Wounds heal and understanding comes with time
Didn't mean to rhyme
But this time I could find
a word of reason.
No need to hide
I am who I am
Not keeping it inside

Solid

I am a mountain
Strong and sturdy
Unmovable
Unconcerned with the wind
Unbothered by the people who
Ascended then descend on me
Scorched by the fire but I still remain
Take it in stride as I withstand the rain
Tall, regal, and sharp
A rough surface
But there to support you through the highs and lows
Chilling but beautiful
it's almost impossible to break your gaze

The Pattern

A work in progress
But I have power in me
Thinking and creativity
Trouble with love
Not practicality
Don't know what I'm missing
Gotta take a deep breath
Can't avoid the risks,
 do what I need to start over again
I say I'm okay, 'cuz they won't get it anyway
Deeply rooted emotions
It's so overwhelming
Suppressed emotions and vulnerability
No, that doesn't come easy for me
Want to consider every possibility
Curious with varied interests
A lot of pressure to pin one down
And narrow my focus
Part of the process
But part of the pain
Nothing to lose
Everything to gain

The Big Blue

I feel clean and refreshed
Enough tears today to fill an Olympic pool
But my heart isn't heavy,
weights have been lifted off my chest

Breaking through the barriers
And addressing the trauma
I feel so much better
and nows the time to leave the drama

You're good where you are, your best yet
You're only going up from here so don't you fret
The signs and messages from God are loud and clear
Continue to serve others and cancel your fears

Those two things will take you far in life
Through the trials and tribulations
The turmoil and strife
The storms and rain won't flood you out
No, there will be no drought
Without a doubt
With the tears that fall, seeds are watered in the ground
You're doing fine now, don't compare your journey
You worry too much, you're not even thirty
Just relax and live your life
Continue to do you
Educate and love yourself
Till your face is blue
No matter the hue
human, you got this
Stand firmly on your ground
don't let anyone plow it

Sunshine

I am me
Beautiful brown eyes
Pretty smile
Warm and welcoming
I love my beauty
But I know that's not all of me
You see,
Deep down
 there's a girl with big bright dreams
And to give back to those in her community
To leave the world better than she found it
To create an impact that's simply timeless
There's a vision
She'll make a way
But I can't say I don't have "those" days
That girl? She used to be bullied, picked on, and teased
Sometimes from her "friends" and mainly her family
Even now she questions her greatness
 and what her true purpose and impact will be
But with prayer, persistence, and pure love
There's nothing she can't do without God above
Seek the answers when things get weary
And she doesn't have it all figured it out
Its still just the beginning

The Hum of Self-Love

Blissful, blissful, dashing wind
The revelations that come from within
The gratification blooms from within the heart
An overwhelming love, a triumphant spark
Purely summer down to my stomach;
entirely warm; abundantly beaming
The love of self, the greatest love of all
Will always be there to catch you for your tragic falls

Breathe

Just breathe
To the top of your lungs
Exhale and let all that ish go
You don't need it
It doesn't serve you
Calm your breath, calms your mind,
Calms your body, heals your soul
You always do what you're told but right now
Break the rules. Relax yourself,
ease your pain; Only you can
Push the air into your stomach, feel it rise
Blow the air out your chest, mouth open, feel it fall
Drop your shoulders, clear your head
Be in the present, treasure that moment
Connect to your Zen, live in it
Massage your third eye, awaken it
Gaze through your beautiful iris'
Melt like butter, taste the freedom
Experience the glow
Now, your heartbeat is slower
the anxiety is over
Do you feel okay? It'll be fine.
Don't forget to breathe through hard times.
Reset, start over, you're far from over
Your time is now, run towards your fears
You're bigger than your worst nightmare
It's not your fault
You are who you are
You do the best you can
You're hip with the trends,
but you don't have to fit in
You never have to be anything you don't wanna be
Say yes, say no, it doesn't matter to me, shouldn't matter to them
It's you in the beginning and it's you at the end
So what's happens between then is for you to intend

Very Respectfully,
Jade E. Leonard

colophon

Brought to you by Wider Perspectives Publishing, care of James Wilson, with the mission of advancing the poetry and creative community of Hampton Roads, Virginia.

See our production of works from ...

Chichi Iwuorie
Symay Rhodes
Tanya Cunningham-Jones (Scientific Eve)
Terra Leigh
Ray Simmons
Samantha Borders-Shoemaker
Bobby K. (The Poor Man's Poet)
J. Scott Wilson (TEECH!)
Charles Wilson
Gloria Darlene Mann
Neil Spirtas
Jorge Mendez & JT Williams
Sarah Eileen Williams
Stephanie Diana (Noftz)
the Hampton Roads Artistic Collective
Jason Brown (Drk Mtr)
Martina Champion
Tony Broadway
Zach Crowe
Ken Sutton
Crickyt J. Expression
Lisa M. Kendrick
Cassandra IsFree
Nich (Nicholis Williams)
Samantha Geovjian Clarke
Natalie Morison-Uzzle
Gus Woodward II
Patsy Bickerstaff
Catherine TL Hodges
Jack Cassada
Dezz

... and others to come soon.

We promote and support the artists of the 757
from the seats, from the stands,
from the snapping fingers and clapping hands
from the pages, and the stages
and now we pass them forth
to the ages.

Check for the above artists on FaceBook, the Virginia Poetry Online channel on YouTube, and other social media.

Hampton Roads Artistic Collective is an extension of WPP which strives to simultaneously support worthy causes in Hampton Roads and the local creative artists.

Made in the USA
Middletown, DE
30 March 2022

63308468R00031